TH1RTE3N HOURS TO FLY

SCHONE BETHAL

ILLUSTRATIONS BY SCHARLAY WINSTENNA

AURAQ

Printed in the Islamic Republic of Pakistan.
Printed: December, 2020
Edition: 1st
ISBN: 978-969-749-059-2
Price: Rs 900 PKR, $09 US

ISLAMABAD, PAKISTAN

raabta@auraqpublications.com | +92-300-0571-530
www.auraqpublications.com. | @AuraqPublications
ISBN : 978-969-749-059-2

"We wish this souvenir will resonate and strike everyone as a reminder of every enigmatic complexity of their hearts, brains and souls profoundly, that played a huge role in their ultimate self exploration and growth"

-schone bethal and scharlay winstenna

CONTENTS

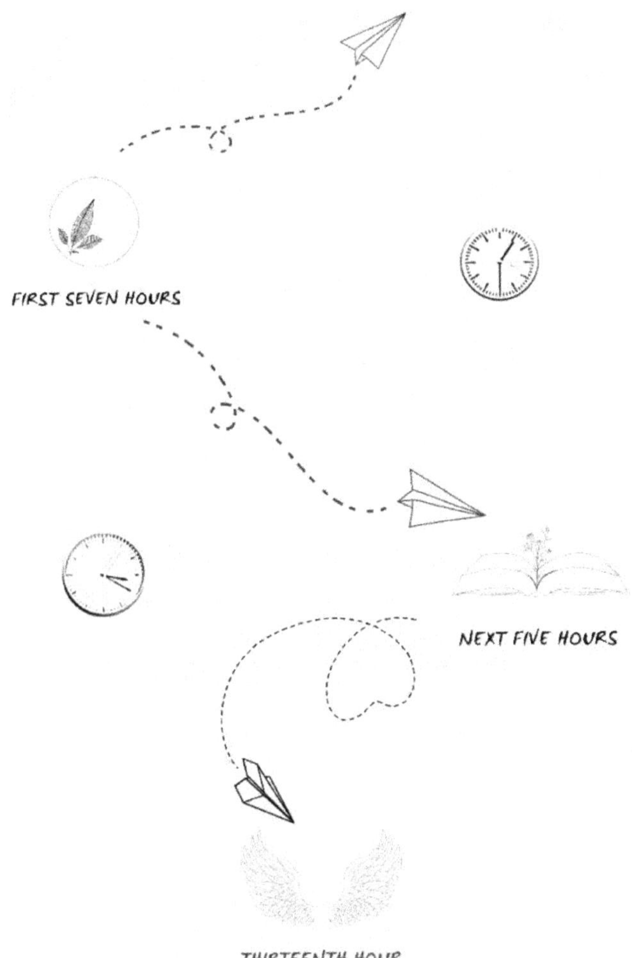

-PROLOGUE-

The soul of our invincible inner universe,

Holds everything together,
Whether constant or on the verge of collapsing,
This soul filled with darkness and terror,
But containing enough stars to shrug the dark matters,

The subtle heart, the subconscious brain,
Both stubborn and sometimes disgrace,
Conjuring miseries and repercussions,
That brings an apocalypse that annihilates every star,

But destruction only imminent,
If the soul succumbs to be numb or tumultuous,
Yet it's nature entirely not destructible,
If it learns to thrive even through storms and thunders,

The soul becomes a revived force,
Of wings and winds to make everything,
Rise stronger beyond the infinity longer,
If peace and patience collude to fonder,

The empty, dimmed and lost soul turns ether,
Brimmed with ultimate light and strength,
Again it also serves the heart and brain that always stumble,
The timeless soul rescues and garners the crumbled.

-we are the ecstatic universe

-schone bethal

FIRST SEVEN HOURS

THE DESTRUCTIVE BEGINNING AND CREATION OF OUR UNIVERSE

THE BIG BANG

Let's begin with beginning of all the drastic beginnings, our universe. Infinitely destructive, known as the Big Bang that lead to this unknown universe, beguiling, shining across dark matter since its creation. Till now endlessly constant, as if it was always there. Still faces destructions and eventually ends up to a peaceful system like ever before and a state of life for every creature. Therefore, now relating to our human nature, that is exactly we know how it works, each day, every second, from every aspect and reality we exist in. We have faced or still face hardships that have had played and are vitally playing the role that are destined to bring the days of hope, joy and tranquility.

Our lives begin the day we think it nearly is on the ultimate end. On the contrary, if we think that our lives ended the day, we thought it just began then we are wrong in each aspect and from every perspective because destructions tend to ambush us every time to renew us, prudently to make us stronger than ever, to imbue us with patience and to make us learn new ways to tackle and prepare us for more that is to come, by embracing the uncertainty. With that only one certain faith it's though possible: WE CAN SURVIVE.

How do we function?

It's so eccentric,
That our hearts,
And our brains,
Work the same way,

Like the moon,
And the sun,
Spin to bring, Dark and Day,

When the heart,
Frightened in the dark,
Dwindling without light,
And sinking away,

But, the brain,
Is inspired to rise,
To be resilient,
And bring a new way.

- schone bethal

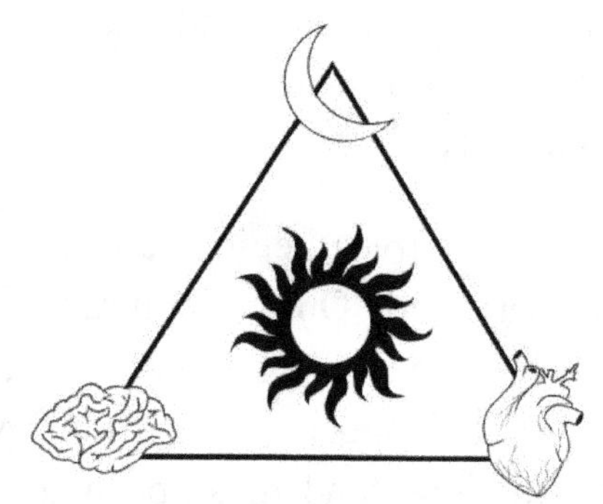

Illustration by scharlay winstenna

RULE OF THE DARKNESS

Since darkness has finally been mentioned, ironically in other words it's our friend, or the balls are in our court to maybe want to call it our lifetime enemy, but is it really our enemy? Embracing it with one major example that it has been there since the creation, it was the first thing to exist before all this existence before every spark of light there was merely dark matter hurdling across the virgin universe, there was doom that prevailed and ruled. In a nutshell, without even a little proportion of darkness, there's nothing that is deemed to begin, shine or to be seen. So, defining and entitling darkness as the 'first input that leads to success and days of eternal light and peace'. Without it we might never comprehend what needs to be enlightened in our universe. Therefore, accepting it in the days of haze is the only way to break out of it, make new ways and to create a whole new ivory universe within us, being constant enough to face the any apocalypse, falling of stars, the sky, everything that stems to product into unbreakable eternal peace.

"nevertheless, what's irrelevant shall always have a part in outshining the relevant"

Importance of darkness:

You wanted eternal light,
And beaming stars,

In your way,

But will the outlines of darkness,
Exist to tell you,

What's the right way?

If you chose you shine,
Every corner,

In your way.

- schone bethal

Illustration by scharlay winstenna

SUBSTAINTIAL ENTITIES THAT PRESERVE THE UNIVERSE

Arriving to things that exist in this vast universe the sun, the moon, galaxy filled with the fulgent and dimmed stars, consistent gravity, dark matter and planets and worlds. These celestial things which hypothetically emphasize mainly as the system of our infernal flesh. The brain, the heart, and most importantly our soul. Dark side of these vulnerable yet fulfilling forces that prevail inside and within us to sustain a solitary kind of connection through which they maintain and prevent falling or a destruction but that does not mean they do not cause apocalyptic eclipses, complexities and storms that are capable of making the gravity of entire universe dwindle and crumble. From the aspect of emphasis, the brain resembling the sun that provides life, provides hope for a light and protects from rotting. Whereas, the subtle heart resembling the moon, gloomy but still needing the support of the brain to survive the darkest nights and change phases to bring the day. The stars, dark matter and persistent gravity resembling the soul, always there, attracting and sparkling within and without. The planets being the people existing under the influence of our mooned-heart, fantasizing, gazing the moon, needing the life of sun, compelled and supported by our universe's stars and undying gravity always holding them. Thus, we are that ecstatic one solitary universe, always ready to renew.

DELICATE CORE OF THE UNIVERSE

Now that it's totally clear that our heart is emphasized with a subtle relation of the moon, always hidden, gloomy, changing phases pretending to be rock solid, filled with scars and wounds but always glimmering even in the deepest of darks similarly like our delicate hearts. The reason it's called the core of our universe is that from all aspects and regardless of every delusional thing it does sometimes being the epitome of stubbornness, it really is the source root of our flesh when it comes to running our inner system, creating blood even when it is dethroned and thwacked by the brain in supremacy just because our heart is delusional and delicate. Although, it is a legitimate fact that the moon requires light of the sun to shine but one fact is inevitable that there is only one mere thing that outcast's darkness and gloom of the night and it's the moon and our hearts. In the worst of days, the heart may stop pumping and numbs due to severe pain and storms of life but eventually it has to renew one way or the other.

For the healing of wounds and scars, the heart does demands and scrounges light to be entered and pain to be abated but not when it realizes that it's kept hidden in its own core and when it outshines through the wounds, they become scars drew with stars. This is how resiliency of the heart helps the soul to move. Portraying the ultimate qualities of being breakable but not invincible because at the end of the horizon, to support and balance our soul. Therefore, it's our heart that succumbs and blindly sacrifices the love and need of light after changing different phases, in chase of the sun, finally to collude with soul to balance the universe. The delicacy is always prominent because of its sacrifice of one and different sides and the need of light to keep shining from that one specific side at the time while another goes in exile. These changing phases of the moon representing the changing of times and inconsistent darkness is something that could be entirely emphasized with the heart as mentioned above apropos to a spiritual connection to maintain peace and internal light from within. The changing of phases is something our heart endures but it could be comprehended in a whole different meaning as well, which is the passage of time and fading of illusionary storms that only invade us to make our core stronger than before. At last, that is how actually the ultimate system or heart is sustainable, through love, chaos and eventually patience.

A cosmic crave of light's bliss:

The darkness of my room,
The gloom of my heart,
Blended together,
Catastrophe, it starts,
Calling forces, from afar,
To enlighten my heart,
The darkness inside and around,
The unhealed wounds cursed,
Wishe to see,
The moon and its lost stars.

- schone bethal

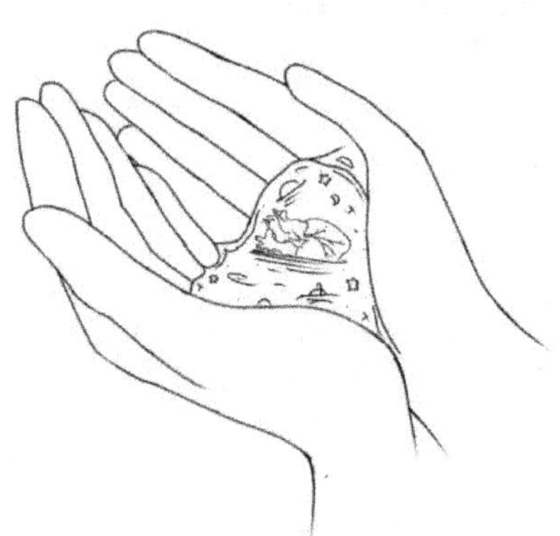

Illustration by scharlay winstenna

Heart that is haunted with soreness:

My abode,
Already is on fire,
With nightmares,
And invisible smokes,
Before the sun rises,
It's cursed,
To set the doors,
And the curtains closed,
The smoke loves to hang around,
Long and trying to choke.

- schone bethal

Illustration by scharlay winstenna

Changing phases of heart like the moon:

These raving circumstances,
Floundering us like it wouldn't extinct,
Staying disguised in the dark,
But ablaze from one side is it's instinct,
Revolving gradually to not mess,
We think it wouldn't rewind,
Changing phases when it's the right time,
Promising an unnerving life,
Hopeless but breath not ceasing an align,
The red skies change portraying resilience,
Even when it's not the day to revive,
With blood flowing in a new rhyme,
Heart break killing like it wouldn't survive,
Changing phases when it's the right time.

-schone bethal

Illustration by scharlay winstenna

Sickening love of heart and nature of the soul:

Uncanny but relatable,
Imperceptible but sickening,
How the waters of land go crazy,
When the moon comes closer,
With its waves touching the dried shores,
The wind blows hard,
Killing the night and morning daisies,
Relatable to me in a way it can be,
Still sickening to my rocked heart,
Dizzy to my deserted stomach,
When you come closer,
The silent beats and the blue blood,
Turns red and rises stronger,
With its waves touching my dried corners,
My existence goes blustery,
Sickening but I love being insane for you.

-schone bethal

Illustration by scharlay winstenna

Sun as the brain and moon as the heart:

The moon got drunk,
With the beauty of the earth,
Now we know,
Why it often appears,
In The day,
I know why it betrays the sun so much,

Our stargaze in the twilight,
Captivating the moons eyesight,
Since the earth sent its witches,
To hex it oh so forever to end the fight,

The sun became brutal,
Now we know,
Why it eclipses quite much,
Being jealous, of this love,
Pretty much.

-irrational love

- schone bethal

Illustration by scharlay winstenna

TWISTED CENTRE OF THE UNIVERSE

It's imminent when we call something twisted; it's the central processing system, the brain emphasized with the utmost relation of the sun. The sun, being the benefactor, the life giver and also the keeper and producer of light keeping everything balanced and alive with its warmth and purpose just like our brain if we ponder profoundly and resonate with the splendid glory of sun. The question is, can something be any superior and unproblematic? Something that does not cause complexities equally to become unhinged and completely deranged to a point where there's only destruction within and without? The answer is straight NO! Because if our central system was unproblematic than we would be just lifeless. Our brain may work on the principles of consciousness and intellectual compatibilities but it has the tendency to eat itself, rot and plague outer places until it has obliterated everything. Emphasizing and relating these quirks to the sun that may be substantial to thrive and keep things preserved but once the heat of sun decides to burn, everything in its way ensures that destruction of fire and there's no stopping but just revival ever after.

"Nothing can destroy iron but its own rust can. Likewise nothing can destroy a human but its own mindset can"

Here, topics such as anxiety and depression could be brought into the limelight because it might be caused by outer force but if we keep that force permeated within the boundaries of our mind with inordinate fear, then we are the ones ourselves to execute something rotting like that. Simultaneously, looking at the other side of the truth in a nutshell, the internal destructions are caused to first destroy and then revive everything that was once resistant or is meant to be after all these twisted games of the mind. Everything existing universe has to experience the raging fires of the sun to live again and again.

Like moth and flame:

Surmising, it's appropriate to start emphasizing depression and our brain with an exquisite example we all might be aware of, MOTH AND FLAME. Our brain loves to grovel around casualties and things that it adores, loves to stay in the thing itself but the reality is that it's impossible. Exactly, caught that right. Let's just believe that anxiety is flame that does not relent itself to be invaded and groveled around by the brain which is certainly a moth, that it even knows the flame is actually dangerous while getting more further and closer by FLYING. That is the point where your brain wants to venture and get into that fire and play with it. Now actually " getting into that fire and play with it " is vividly the events that our brain thinks and believes it can dare to execute but it never thinks that it will eventually be destroyed by the fire that was tempting but not life giving. The subtle wings are now burnt and it will only affect the entire flesh to endure the affects of fire. If this isn't a perfect and most adequate example of anxiety and brain then what is.

Fatal temptations:

Our twisted brain lures to make us feel stained even when we are not. It relentlessly tries to wipe and clean our soul even when it is clear as crystal, filled with hidden light. Likewise, when we feel your hands smudgy while holding something even when they are not, we keep on cleaning the hands to make sure but we end up again in the same situation all over. Now, WE CAN is the mantra and may be a metaphor that only your subconscious mind can decide to let you rely on it and most of us do agree to that. That is precisely called to have a control on your mind. Clicked something? Yes we all did without a question. For example, we do learn to have a peculiar kind of control over something we love or may be a person we love, even though they are the source of our happiness and because of them we are still resilient. But, at a certain point of life We do have the right to argue with them for something that is being wrongly done and to be very honest, not to offence, some do leave and some do stay to listen to us even if they do deem our opinions insignificant but they have the conscience to think about it and prudently give us the right that yes WE CAN counsel them. Therefore, this may be the exact way our soul's relationship with our brain actually works like.

Anxiety:

It's true what they say,
It's not just fear,
That they despair,
And bear,
They are reviving each time,
And killing themselves away,
Why do I know?
Why do I bear?
 It's true what they say,
 That the criminal,
Returns to the place of crime,
And bear,
But I killed myself there,
And again revive,
I bail myself each day,
When the tornadoes of fear,
Bring me there,
To die in a prison,
For someone's blames,
I am deceived to believe,
That I am stained,
Swim without knowing the way,
To a shore or someplace
Repeating everything,
Relentlessly to stay.

-crimes of the brain

- schone bethal

Illustration by scharlay winstenna

Dear brain:

We seed hope
In our minds,
Unaware of the soil,

But the roots grew,
To be terrors,
And frights,

I think we watered it,
With hounding fear,
Ambiguous, with frail ice.

-schone bethal

Illustration by scharlay winstenna

When the soul arrives to rescue every time:

The brain ambushes,
The frail heart,
When it's on the verge to bloom,
With glory of every petal,
Patronizing with light,
Urging to high rise,
And untangle the storms of the mind,
The heart flounders,
The blood that flows waste,
Needed for all the flowers and stars,
The mind puts all the blame,
Nested in disdain now,
Ready to con the heart that it failed,
Caved in exile,
Courage the heart still ignites,
Power of the soul enters, it's divine,
Pouring the heart and restoring the light,
Such is the alluring connection,
Soaring whenever one is falling apart,
The sacrifice for each other,
Thrives till the end of the times a far.

-there for each other every time.

-schone bethal

Illustration by scharlay winstenna

Seizing happiness, ceasing happiness:

The voids in our brains,

Leak persistently,
When happiness is poured,
It deems to invade at its will,
Yet swiftly it spills,
It's tends to be a guest,
Leaving back empty rooms,
Without any rest,
Leaving rooms for sorrows and pains,
Which don't deem to leave swiftly?
They plague and stay.

- schone bethal

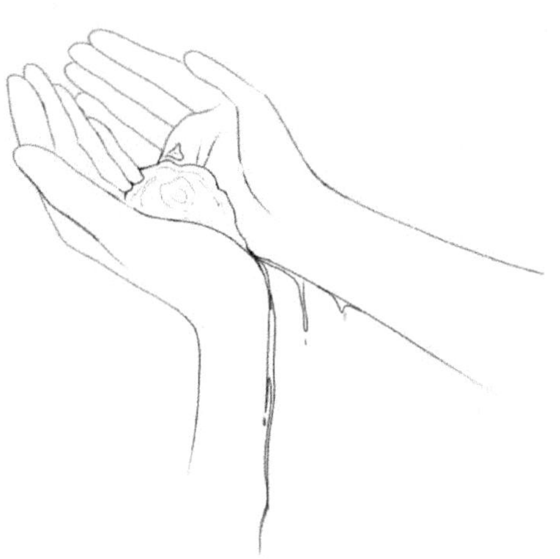

Illustration by scharlay winstenna

Delicate solidarity of the brain:

I'm that,
Resistant wall,
That always,
Stands still,

I'm wrapped with a skin,
To not show,
That from inside,
I can be delicate and ill.

- schone bethal

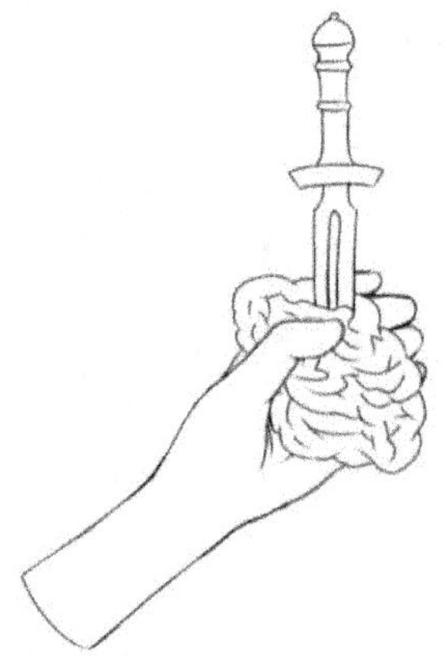

Illustration by scharlay winstenna

Other side of the shunned brain:

I was the beguiling sunset,
Everyone enjoyed and praised,
But cursed and bailed,
Which I couldn't refrain,
When they ceased to see,
My fulgent stars shining with wisdom,
For them in the hounding dark,
They wished a certain sun again,
With their fear of a dark night,
That I didn't begin,
Could've ended without vain,
Where I had the power,
To diminish the lurking pain,
By bringing the day again,
Yet no one had the power,
To realize and accept,
Those things don't remain the same,
I am a shunned light now,
Lurking to seek eyes,
I am no more the day.

-schone bethal

Illustration by scharlay winstenna

WRATHS OF OMINOUS BLESSINGS:

There's a notion which states "blessings in disguise", is that really a certain sort of belief? Or a metaphoric self help phrase to sustain the sole nature of faith and hope in oneself? What is it really? When we muse about ominous blessings, it's evident that it's a prelude of an event or tragedy, either currently occurring or it has already befallen upon us. Precisely, something that is malevolently threatening and destructive but in such a disguise that gives us the ultimate feeling of something that really bad is about to happen, and it actually does. What exactly is the point of calling it a blessing in disguise? Does that particularly specifies time that was hounding us, which abruptly turns out to be in favor of us benevolently? The answer to that is found when we really endure something and realize that it was for a reason, for our betterment even if there was pain in it. The mere idea is the passage of time and how it is meant to change us.

This universe faces a lot of wraths, and eventually it's for the betterment of the universe itself each day. Things are destroyed but on the other hand they are also reborn in a new way and given a new life. Having said that, this is the way and process of how infinite the universe is and will be apropos to its relation and emphasis with our souls that live to renew each day and by every collapse. Only on one single notion that everything happens for a certain reason even if it is uncertain before. With this notion, we can comprehend the nature of uncertainty as well because accepting it is a great deal not everyone can strike to bargain with.

2020:

This year has been a roller coaster ride, and when it's called a roller coaster ride the chances are that there have been and still a plethora of unreal incidents while riding on that roller coaster and not few but in every up and down there was an another up and down. Precisely, a severe dizziness that has misplaced everyone's existence every dimension and aspect, upside downed our minds, hearts and souls. Everything torn apart with adverse speed and eventually thrown away in an exile lost and far away from light not able to reach our eyes, blinding us, making us naive and and numb. Noises of everyday silenced in the gravitating thunderstorms, deafening the ears. Brain, heart and soul, all untenable enough survive.

Ostentatiously, looking from the other side, 2020 pandemic and isolation of the world has been a blessing in disguise. It's entirely onerous to fathom this fact but deep down we all know how we have thrived throughout spiritually while being in a literal exile whereas the world was on a collapse. We always complained to not find adequate time and peace to rest and spend it with our close ones, but this time it came to fruition in a totally unprecedented way. Our hearts were healed, the restless and distressed minds accessed a lot of peace, and the lost souls were found, locked and refreshed. Eventually, we are ready to embrace it when we all finally endured it, as mentioned above about the passage of time and that there's no way we can be stuck in a time loop forever. Hence proved that everyone happens for a reason if there's embracing in it, even if the other side of the reality may be ominous and threatening, it too shall pass.

APOCALYPSES AND REVIVAL OF THE SOUL:

"in the end, after every sabotage and storm, it's the nature that returns to rule. Likewise, our soul after it renews."

Returning back to the emphasizing narrative of our universe again. Far away, deep down in our universe, in our flesh, in our own intellect, there always exist the black holes, always scrounging to destroy and eat the galaxies we have build the planets and accumulated safely in your heart's core. There's always this one demon existing in our subconscious mind, which hounds us to sporadically over think and destroy the deep rooted hopes and task we are on the due to complete and bring to fruition. The bitter truth is that we cannot run away from those demonic black holes when they themselves are gravitated and attracted by us. The only way to defeat them is to stay resilient and combat every battle, to prevail and cope up with every consequences that are imminent There's a certainty, we can dodge those black holes from devouring your peace and light only when you have enough courage and audacity that forged our soul to be invincible enough to prevent a destruction that actually makes you ride on the road leading to peace and happiness, only when we have reckoned out the right paths to travel and not on those of fatal temptations.

Verily, these inner demonic destructions, stem from within, ostensibly. It's the only thing that exposes us to the ultimate states of depression and self-undermining. Subsequently, halting every process we were confident about but not any self destruction also comes under the theory of the Big Bang, where we are actually learning self control this time, self empowerment this time to be invincible and permeate light. Yes, we all got it right that the spell of Anxieties can be broken. Our life is reflection of ever thing that unknowingly began and embracing it relevantly helps us co-exist with every being and system of life. We might defy out reality some times, but it is what is and it will be how we tend to survive it with balance of understanding the beginning of everything and to not focus on the end that is always uncertain and unpredictable. Further, this book will guide us thoroughly how to cope up and how to not surrender to the events that always befell for a reason, or the things that exist for a reason with a relation of narratives of natural systems of our beliefs and disbeliefs we choose to embrace and omit.

Lost were the times but found are the hearts:

Sole must have been these chaotic times,
Only if they could really affect our souls,
Well they could be if we stay stuck in the past or inside,
Promising was only the fear,
But we still have hands to hold and fight along and stand,
To combat while growing together but still it felt all lonely and sad,
Uncertain were the hopes,
With no loss but a lot of regret,
Only if we were in this alone,
The world appeared to collapse,
But now the sheer reality appears to be not like that,
It's the chaos intervening our voided minds and bleeding hearts,
Solemn was the mission to survive,
But new tragedies brew to tear us while obliging us to grow inside,
It was the chance and a certainty to thrive,
There must've not been raving happiness,
We think we must be losing time,
The truth is that ominous blessings ambush us when we love to hide,
The clouds might the silver lining are near,
But the wait is grooving our skin with golden lines of despair,
Bright will be the colors of this exile if we are resilient to stay,
Making us prone to endure more and realize,
That some things come to bring a change be it storms of thorns or,

Mere is an escape with the pouring of thunder, roses and
shrines,
Assure a hope to feel but to not just see,
In This coming time of feasts,
A revival of hearts, souls and minds is indeed.

(A Souvenir of new revival from 2020)

-schone bethal

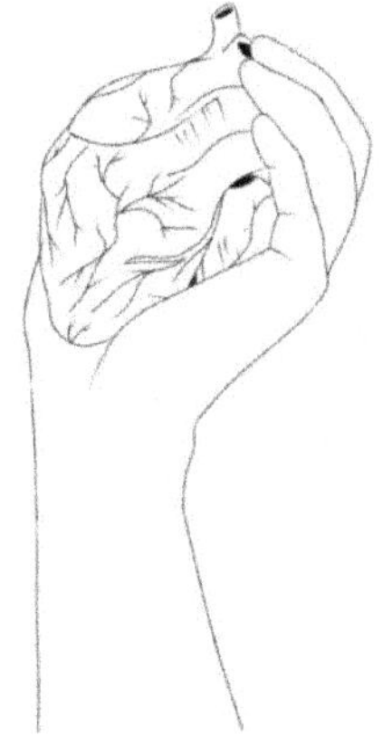

Illustration by scharlay winstenna

How do we live?

I thought people end their lives,
With a notion,
To run away,
And enter another realm,

I Pierce my nerves,
All day, every time,

It produces hundreds of worlds,
So beautiful,
Giving me refuge and chance to stay,

My world still didn't end,
They grow inside to keep me awake.

- schone bethal

Illustration by areeba sarwar

Loops of time:

Not again the time,
Not again the cruelty,
Is repeated,
But even if it does,
2021 would be a fun ride,
Promising new attempts,
Ticking the right answers that time,
On the deadly quiz,
We were tempted to fail, In the midst of the time,
But prevailed to learn,
And sneak on the correct answers,
Carved on the heart that time,
Yearning to bleed again,
From the dry scratches,
Of this boundless, time.

-schone bethal

Refuge in the soul:

Walking out of time,
Looking for a space,
Where I can live that one moment,
Forever with no shame,
And cease to return,
Back to the terrifying haze.

-refuge in a different time loop

- schone bethal

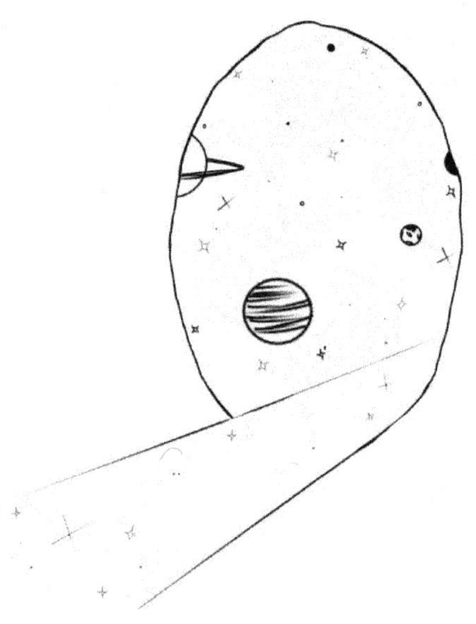

Illustration by scharlay winstenna

Unbridled enduring of the soul and promises of time:

It takes time,
Time to change,
The time,

But why,
Why do we love?
The pain,

That brings,
Brings about a life,
Dead but alive,

We hate,
Hate the time,
We blame it,

Instead our love,
Love for the pain,
That never nudged us.

Kept the home fire,
Burning the frozen time,
Keeping things to someday shine.

-schone bethal

Illustration by scharlay winstenna

The flesh and the eternal soul:

I am the ocean,
With the waters,
Brimmed with my tears,

It's weird to ask,
This time the water,
Need your plants, to soak my tears.

My soul would be purified,
With the bliss,
And aroma, that will clear the fears.

-schone bethal

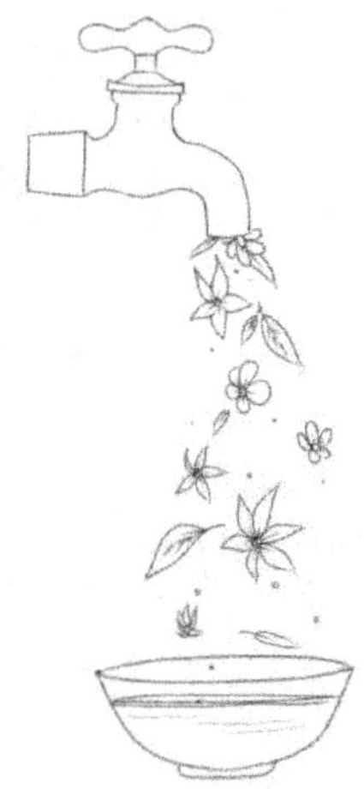

Illustration by scharlay winstenna

Dear emptiness of the soul:

We loved a little hope,
Only when we highly soared,

We dodged loneliness,
When we knew it'd sneak in and haunt,

We sought happiness,
When we knew it would leak and fall.

-schone bethal

Falling forces of our realm:

Who knew the direction?
When their heart,
Flew in the air,
Who saw the way?
When their minds,
Created haze,
But, who knew,
Both didn't knew,
How to swim in the ocean,
Rising because of the heart,
In regret and tears.

- schone bethal

Illustration by scharlay winstenna

When one seeks a revival:

New beginnings,
Began to become,
Like My new religion,

The places I see every day,
Began to accept me,
Ready to be my new abodes,

This melting soul begins,
To wonder and move,
Like My wandering feet that's cold,

A piece of darkness still in me,
Persists to stop me,
Like My heart will never cease to beat.

This new itinerary,
Begins to remind me everything,
Like My Old self never did,

By only trudging forward,
Opening the eyes and hands,
Would've only helped.

-schone bethal

Illustration by scharlay winstenna

Phases of masks:

This Ivory of masks,
Clinging to skin,
These few phases circling,
Hiding the sick like it's a sin,
This irony of masks,
These many faces hurdling,
Surviving so hard like it's a win,
Empty Sky now not the same,
But with hope,
For arrival of a new phase,
Empty Land now not the same,
But bringing a new chase,
Of the stars,
Of the chaos,
In the dark,
In the evil,
These stars falling from above,
But these hardships brew from beneath,
The sky clear may not be so clear to see,
Running and distancing here is the greed,
Protecting one is protecting all indeed,
In form of a curse,
A blessing has ambushed,
Drenched us with darkness,
But a light to chase and retrieve,
Cunning are the voices,
Of the obsessions we crave and seed,
These masks, These phases,
Have halted everything,
Instead of our growth,
And uncertain beliefs.

-schone bethal

Illustration by scharlay winstenna

Immortality of the soul:

They thought,
I was building fences,
Scared of the world,

To cope, my foreseen craze.

I believed,
I built fences,
To keep myself inside,

To escalate, my unseen glaze.

-a substantial exile

-schone betha

Illustration by scharlay winstenna

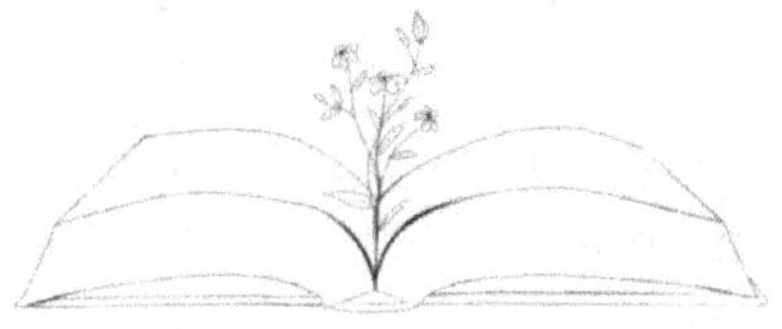

NEXT FIVE HOURS

THE EXPLORATION AND
GROWTH OF HUMAN NATURE

EMBRACING OF UNCERTAINTY

A great writer once said "Perhaps the Earth was made round so that we would not see too far down the road."

It's true actually, because knowing and being certain about what is going happen or where we are going to end up wouldn't just make any sense at all because we already walk in fear on that road uncertain of everything. Walking is important, so is being afraid, because it means we are ready to keep moving no matter what obstacles and storms comes in between that road to make us fall or run back. Now embracing that 'certain' uncertainty can cost us anything but that acceptance wholly nurtures and prepares us to battle and not surrender. It's grueling to keep moving in the haze unknown of the terrors but it's also not okay to sit in the haze, nodded down and wait for the haze to vanish. At last, it's the illusionary confusion that manipulates us to give up and the balls are in our court to either succumb to the illusions or stand up by escalating the forces of faith and hope and start walking. In spite of everything, uncertainty is always vitally important to cram and overflow all the voids that occur in dire circumstances or the days full of light and bracing. The subtle reason why uncertainty is as important as anything in keeping the faith and belief in disappearance of darkness, persistently, is to believe in opting risks and falls that may end up leading us into our peaceful rendezvous we never thought would be in front of us after all that we had excruciatingly bared. To be consistent about that one thought of REVIVAL AFTER A HARSH FALL is to endure and jump for that fall rather than to sit, conjure haze, darkness, numbness and everything that prevents us to proceed exceedingly. Therefore, the more we think about getting hurt the more that over thinking hurts us worse because it relentlessly staggers us back to take a new step. It escalates and turns the fear into attributes of coward and guilt. The purpose of uncertainty is to merely be unapologetic to ourselves in every way and dimension so that self confidence and self determination impels and wheels us to endure the pain and to not stupidly sit in despair about the coming conflict.

Eternal faith:

Some sobbed,
Failed, gave up,
When saw,
The Clouds came,
Thundering and escalating their fear,
Without the silver lining,
While others,
Enlightened themselves,
From the ruins,
Of their fallen stars,
And enlightened,
Their hazed and dimmed ways.

- schone bethal

Illustration by scharlay winstenna

Hung to catch a life:

In The arid winds,
To The harness,
That I'm clinging,

Can't help me,
Dry the pain,
but I'm enduring,

It's still frozen blue,
The sun doesn't helps,
But I'm melting.

I'm solid it feels like,
But also falling under the blue sky,
And I'm also failing.

- schone bethal

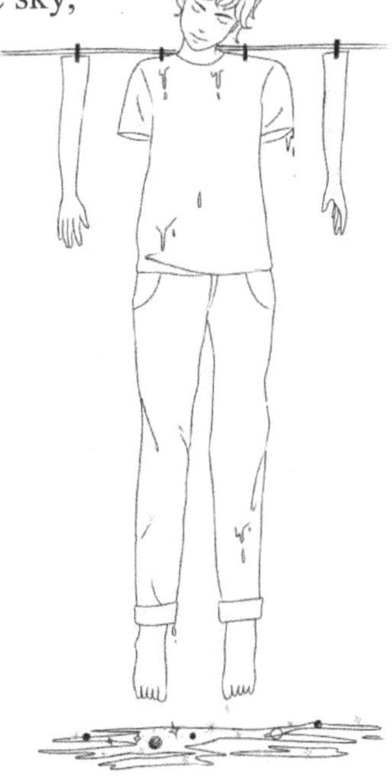

Illustration by scharlay winstenna

An exhilarating growth:

Been Growing,
Inside, Concealed,
To outshine,
One day, brighter,

Still waiting,
To bloom,
To be unlocked,
Sometime, higher,

I'm desperate,
To be unfurled,
To show,
Someone, fire,

Until a force,
To break me,
To make me,
Dark and liar.

- schone bethal

Illustration by scharlay winstenna

Confused but a believer:

In This solitude,
Up above,
I'm locked beneath,
The ocean of a rainless sky,

I thought this sun,
Would turn me,
Numb and sore,
I was telling myself a lie,

Laid down,
Blinding my eyes,
The agony,
Healed with the burns of fire,

I'm painting myself Golden,
Glitter, a few,
Letting the scars shine,
I was dumb to not let go the blue.

I realized I can be a rainbow,
Shining across,
Giving hope,
I'll be rare and divine.

- schone bethal

Illustration by scharlay winstenna

Our shooting scars:

Tears and stars,
Having semblance,
Above the deserted deserts,

Shooting, when happy,
Or when the hearts were tearing apart,

Attracted millions,
But resembled only the ones,
Who were in the same dark?

Putting a scar,
Leaving the marks,

Waiting to be washed away,
For the eclipse and floods,
Upon, the dark skies and scars.

- schone bethal

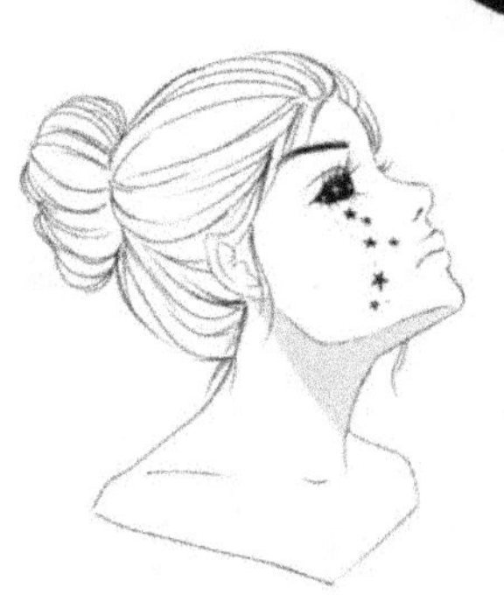

Illustration by scharlay winstenna

Dark but energizing:

I was bewildered,
If it were the foamy waves,
Touching my feet,
Or the rebellious clouds,
Showering salted tears,
Extracting my evaporating sentiments,
Because sitting upside down,
Watching my reflection was a creed,
It was bright that time,
Or I was just simulating the moon,
Or the moon reflecting,
My eternal but dimmed beam,
Where I stood like an island between,
Cursed with silence,
That was doomed to sink,
But Ready to rise,
The night saved me,
It brought life to my concealed light,
The sadness that was poured,
Travelled upwards in a fleet,
My Darkness,
Became a sacrifice indeed.

-schone bethal

Illustration by scharlay winstenna

Cursed:

I'm still blinded,
By my own eyes,
Those are open,
And cannot close to hide,

Because they bleed black,
Instead of dripping,
They travel,
And freeze back.

- schone bethal

Illustration by scharlay winstenna

Depression:

Can my heart beat?
Be louder,
To disturb the outer world,
And let know?
Because,
It doesn't stops,
Shaking my inside a with flow,
Creating worlds of sorrows,
Chaos that turns me coal,
Unless silence ambushes,
But still,
It ceases to show,
My flesh,
Doesn't knows how to volume up,
It's queer and always low.

-how do we express the distress?

- schone bethal

Illustration by scharlay winstenna

Pain and injustice:

I'm that rootless,
Flower,
Burning,
Yearning for a shower,
There's no love,
I need incandescent power,
My petals fall,
I have no bower,
Can someone just pluck me?
To end this raging fighter,
Standing still like an heir,
Searching for something,
That no one can answer.

- schone bethal

Illustration by scharlay winstenna

Everything needs freedom:

I'm fed up,
Of sticking my neck out,
To sneak myself out
Through the cages of hell,

Why is my soul, rushing,
Out of my flesh,
It doesn't rests and sleeps so well,

Am I a cage?
Like this world also a cage?
Can they be broken?
Does that means that they fragile like a shell?

- schone bethal

Illustration by scharlay winstenna

When we sat inside and the world changed:

May be we mistake,
This salt air with a sweet haze,
That we have exhaled,
Unable to escape out,
Absorbing back in our bones,
Making them more strain,
To not stand up and thrive,
Out of this bubble in disguise,
Mistaken for a protection,
From a fear of getting erased,
Decisive to not see,
Deceived by our own faulted,
Hindered brain,
Causing to dwindle oneself,
While the outside world,
Has been cleared.

-schone bethal

Illustration by scharlay winstenna

Women of the golden hour:

She grew fire on her head,
But she settled the storms,
Unsettling the ambush of waters,
With her celestial hands capable of turning to west.

She pardoned,
Her light,
But the drowning night couldn't,
Save the defying lands collapsing in raving mess.

- Invincible glory

- schone bethal

Illustration by scharlay winstenna

A mother:

She's the one,
The divine and sublime,
Her nature is the nature itself,
She's the one giving birth,
To every life that dwells,
Her presence bless our insights,
Her morning glory arouses,
Shone her hidden golden sparks,
Her hair diffracting a scene,
Of Resilience and courage,
That outcasts the utmost sunlight,
Of every glimmering day,
That gets dim and isn't enough,
Showcasing her Goddess avatar,
And raving sides creating rays,
Her scars of what she has dealt,
Turned into songs and melodies,
Printed on her flawless skin of the flesh,
She holds a universe in her eyes,
Her heart softens and melts,
Her feet containing heaven,
But her rage can conjure hells,
Silencing the horns,
But can protect from every wrath.

-a descended entity

-schone bethal

Illustration by scharlay winstenna

Uncertainty in trying:

Standing on the verge of a cliff,
No doubt, isn't any scarier,
Than actually sky diving,
Without the clipped wings,
That needed force to open,
When we assumed,
That the wind,
Wouldn't even accept it.

-schone bethal

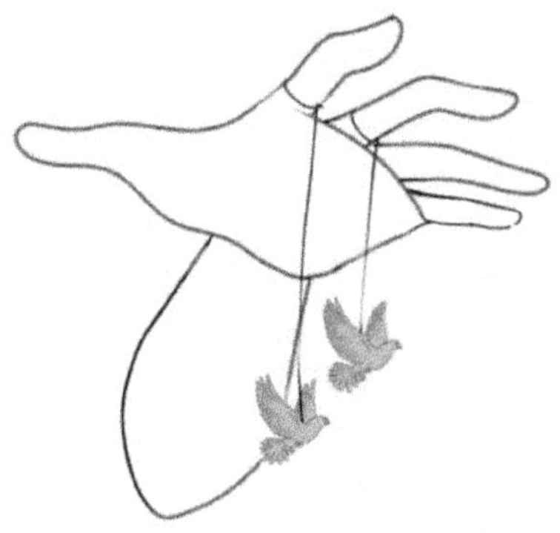

Illustration by scharlay winstenna

Reasons and predestinations:

Sometimes things don't work,
They way we might have expected,
Because it was best for us,
Even if it thwacked us and drifted,
Not back to the same,
But a new kind of drawing board.

-schone Bethal

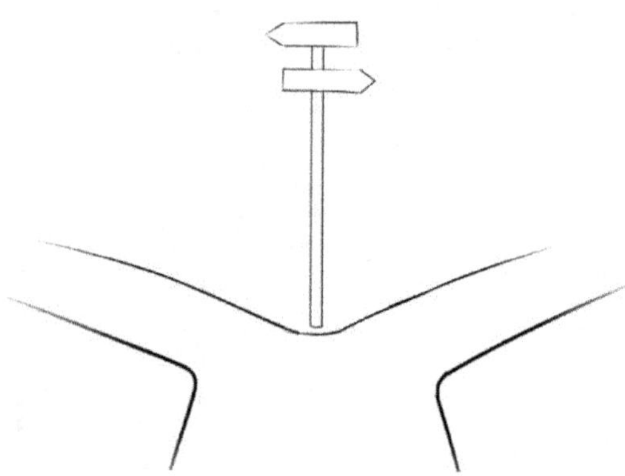

Illustration by scharlay winstenna

Killing agony kills:

l Thought was I searching,
For myself,
To find the answer,
To this agony,
I learnt I was hurting,
Myself,
I was still stuck,
Escalating this agony,

The tasks so hard,
For me,
To leave back my heart,
To be free,
I learnt I was betraying,
Myself,
I will still be there again,
Shunned by the pain.

-schone bethal

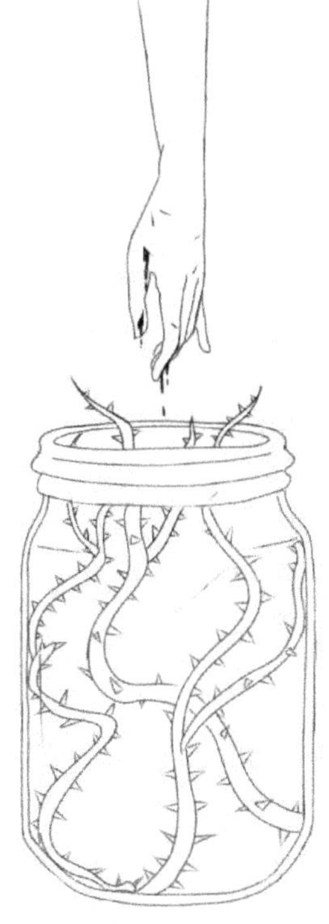

Illustration by scharlay winstenna

Self help:

However would we know?
How long, how rough,
How light, how heavy,
If pieces of our personality,
For once weren't broke,
To become solid again,
From the tarnish and storms,
Putting each one back,
Being clueless on the glue-less spots,
With a fear what if they fall back,
The skin color withered and tanned,
With marks of past scars and cracks,
Destroyed but meant to be back,
Again into a new spiraled flesh,
Destruction becomes a reason,
To revive oneself,
And discover self help.

-bits and pieces brought back

-schone bethal

Illustration by scharlay winstenna

Dear patience:

What is this wait?
Wait that kills but also fills me,
With a hope and light,
That far away couldn't be seen,

What is this feel?
Feel that it's going to bring something,
Lost but written for me,
That will be left for me to be seen,

News of love,
Secret Recipe of a pain killer,
That could be used to light,
And heal the scars that still bleed.

-schone bethal

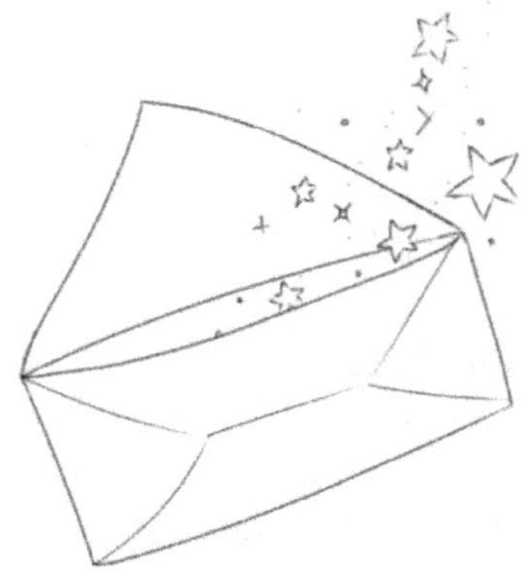

Illustration by scharlay winstenna

Secret shades and freedom fades:

I tried to escape,
On one shade,
I fell and failed,
The heart parades,
To accept the hidden,
Ride on all the shades,
These broken wings,
Forcibly stained,
Yearning to unfurl in the air,
Like an independent,
Vibrant flag,
But not just red,
When how the secrets would fade,
I'll be free,
From the grey haze,
That blurred my existence,
I'll just escape,
Rescue myself,
Into another world,
If this one didn't cared,
If one shunned,
At last, I'll be in the clear,
Above the fake,
My secrets shall escalate,
Into a reality,
Of my own divergent ways.

-schone bethal

Illustration by scharlay winstenna

Disbeliefs and deceiving:

Why do these lights form a direction?
In my way,
When I am still lost in those lights,
I cease to see any way.

- schone bethal

Illustration by scharlay winstenna

Light can be torturing:

My shadows became vague,
The surreal light behind me,
Above me, beside me,
That I adored for centuries,
I was soaking in for days,
One day, I came,
To let it show my real face,
It didn't show me my Rays,
It drew my shadow on a wall,
Burning for its sake,
It told me, it screamed,
That my soul is stale,
It told me,
I was shallow and empty,
And I was dark and fake.

-schone bethal

Illustration by scharlay winstenna

Locking ourselves:

The doors of my closet,
Were jubilant,
When I opened,
Thought I had come,
To dress free,
Unlock that was closed inn,
Yet I slammed,
And instead locked myself,
Behind these doors,
That I could see,
Threw the key outside,
To rot inside,
My stranded closet,
But I'm sleeping the light,
I was supposed to shine with,
Out of this Darkness and Creep.

-schone bethal

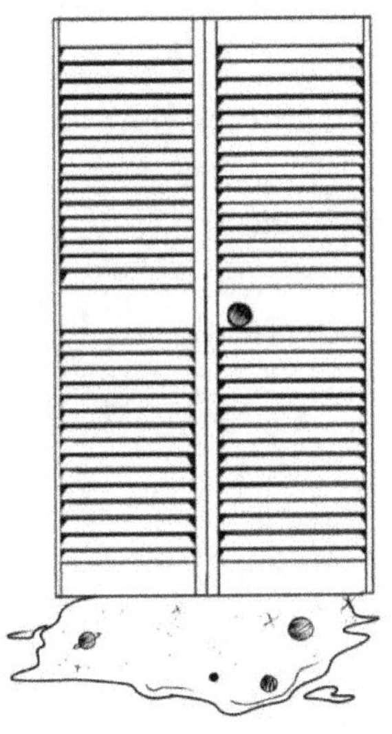

Illustration by scharlay winstenna

Dear vengeance:

The day my flesh,
Halts to ignite,
The flames,
That burnt my soul,

Is the day?
I begin to become,
A sterling storm,
That ruins the cores,

That obliterated,
Tarnished and dried,
My oceans of soul,
From the cores,

I wish to banish,
My light,
For a time,
Bring fruition a burning role.

-schone bethal

Illustration by scharlay winstenna

Dear spontaneous feelings:

Do you sometimes think,
While sitting alone,
From the window,
Gazing at the luminous night sky,
Patronizing but for a short time,
But exerting a peace,
That the day couldn't provide,
With the light just shines,

Do you sometimes think,
While crying alone,
On a shoulder,
Of someone you don't know,
Lasting but for a
short time, But
relieving the inner
pain,
That couldn't happen with
someone, You knew for a
long while.

-schone Bethal

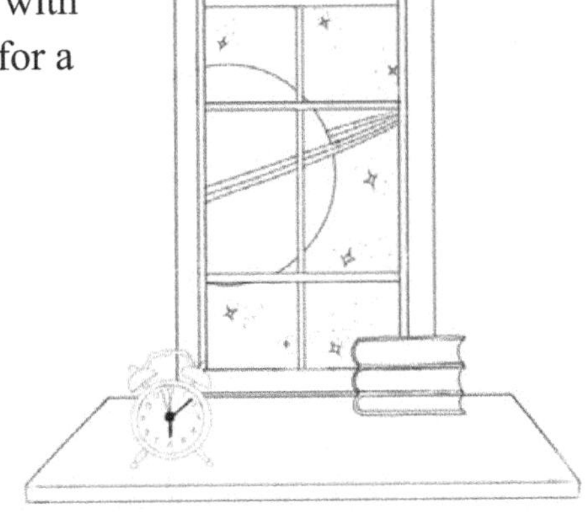

Illustration by scharlay winstenna

Thought I'd make it better but I couldn't:

Kept running with numb celerity,
Stabbing the bosky land,
Combating with the thwacking whirls of winds,
With my Echoing feet,
That actually beseeched,
To bless the cursed lands,
Thought my falling grief,
Sorrow would grow a paradise of peace,
With the rain of my crystal tears,
That falls when I run and seed,
Yet they grew into thorns,
To kill and curse me instead,
I wish in upside down underworld,
In an alternate reality of this world,
I'm growing vibrant florets,
Enough to make things beautiful,
Alright, content and bloom.

-thought I would make it better but I couldn't

-schone bethal

Illustration by scharlay winstenna

Scared of theft:

I'll let, the wind,
Take away,

The feelings,
That I wear,

As a fragrance,
Of undying love and rays,

Before someone else arrives,
Attracted to my shades

And steals them,
To use and play.

- schone bethal

Illustration by scharlay winstenna

Blessings of a voice:

I've been painting,
The air,
With soundless songs,

The lost souls found a way,
Through it,
They've become strong,

The Wrecks,
The destroyed,
Have unraveled along,

Everything is rejoicing,
With the winds,
I blew with soundless songs.

- schone bethal

Illustration by scharlay winstenna

Dear fear:

I am pirate of my own ship wreck,
And you came like the perfect storm,
While I was carrying a broken heart,
While not believing in rain,
Yet your storm came to ambush instead,
It was actually you eagerly waiting,
Right I guessed,
Before the killing sun arose,
Its light I sought that lessened my pain,
But your dark motive of all,
In this dead night of cold,
Was merely to break something,
That was already broken,
It held a few things left with hope,
it wasn't withered, suffering alone,
Deeper than the ocean,
But still Breathless,
Clinging to find its shore of stay,
But you knew the possessions,
That's why arrived with silence,
In the midst of this unknown way,
To annihilate these sources,
With unbound secrets,
That could defeat your fame.

-schone bethal

Illustration by scharlay winstenna

A criminal:

Disappointment,
Is the biggest thief,
It steals and runs away,
With every hope and dream,
From a person,
That was rooted deep.

- schone bethal

Illustration by scharlay winstenna

Mistaken:

Just like some things,
Merely fill the stomach,
But, have no energy to give,

Some people,
Only fill the voids of heart,
Yet, have no love to give.

- schone bethal

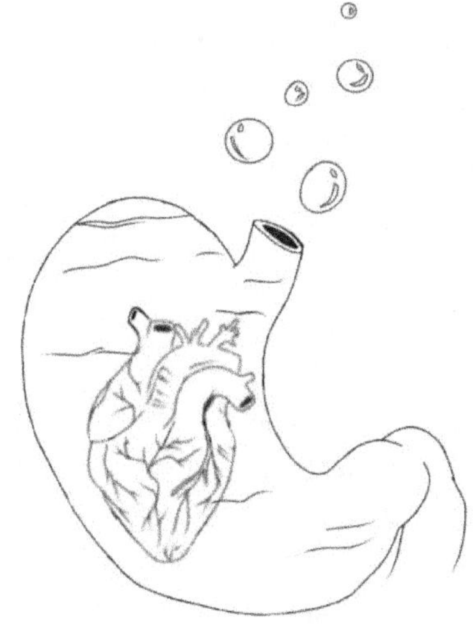

Illustration by scharlay winstenna

Pillows of the willows:

These pillows,
Be it any rough side,
Giving eternal comfort,
Ready to soak,
The Deep pain of my willows,
No sides promises a betrayal,
A want or a leave,
Or to lie and a greed,
Buying me sleep,
Costing nothing for soaking my grief,
Producing a lullaby,
These pillows pretend to be the artists,
Of the hallowed violins cursed with silence,
That were once thrown and hidden,
Under the willows,
But meant for the wounds of our ears,
Bleeding with the treachery, and pain,
Burnt with the lies and craze,
Instead of turning me coal,
But pale as yellow they absorbed my sore,
These pillows ivory and white,
They paint my hidden bruised scars,
Beneath the skin of my head with gold,
Blended with the it's magic for a time,
The cruelty of the day would still,
Hurt the skin and fill the eyes,
With crippling heaviness,
And darkness of our sorrowed willows.

-schone bethal

Illustration by scharlay winstenna

Setting examples:

Your little bruises,
Don't need any light,
They hurt you,
But they aren't wounds,

They need,
To be embraced,
To show,
The scars of lessons and doom,

That you survived,
To Have enough light inside,
To differ,
What is fake and true?

-schone bethal

A sacred poem:

I was the poem,
Everyone refused to read,

Dodged the secrets,
Written on me,

I was the product,
Of catastrophes,

They said I faked the pain,
Rhyming on me.

-schone bethal

Illustration by scharlay winstenna

Vulnerable:

Held my emptied self,
With my bare hands,
Wished I would gather,
And turn it into a new flesh,
But it wasn't as empty,
And alluringly or clear,
It escaped faster,
Than the air,
Trapped in my rock lungs,
In disguise of sand,
That keeps me dead but awake,
To remind my halted heart, That I can't rescue,
Or ever renew myself.

-schone bethal

Illustration by scharlay winstenna

Bewitched by the killing light:

Look through the dark,
The truth it tells you,

The stories of light,
Have always deceived you,

Why do you embrace the harsh reality?
To, be fine with you.

- schone bethal

Sometimes it's better to be numb:

Holding the source,
Of my extra breath,
In case I drift off,
For eternity in the breathless haze,
My eyes hid by the sunflowers,
I carry or that I grew instead,
To keep them averted,
From the temptations,
That may burn this flesh,
But there exist enough florets,
Rooted Within me,
Of that I am unaware,
They grow with smooth celerity,
To not let me feel the harsh pains,
Because Even if they are plucked,
I am destined,
To not feel the agony,
But move on an unseen way.

-schone bethal

Illustration by scharlay winstenna

Co-existing realms of nature:

The clouds,
Tasted like my salty tears.
They had soaked my tasteless heart,
When I flew to them with clipped wings,
They consoled me by silencing my pain,
Under their cool hays,
They felt pity for me,
But they saw a burning ocean in me,
They promised,
To take revenge for me,
With the thunders and rain of my tears,
To thwack whatever that ruined me.

-our connection with the sky

-schone bethal

Illustration by scharlay winstenna

Thirst of true lies:

Fluttering butterflies,
In clear skies,
Of emptiness,
Needing, blind eyes,

Fluttering butterflies,
In full bellies,
Of sadness,
Needing, true lies.

- schone bethal

Illustration by scharlay winstenna

Our complicated nature:

We were wondering,
Wondering to be fire,
Fire in a world,
A world that keeps getting colder,
We pretend to be fire fighters,
Yet we still get burned.

-schone bethal

Bliss of the art:

Grateful to the art,
It lets us vent,
The emotions,
Welled up,
Picturing beyond,
The impossible,

For a return back,
The art never complained,
It fills us and empties us,
At the same time,
It loves to be graced,

Out of the brain and on a page,
To be rugged,
It fulfills the bliss,
And never complains.

-schone bethal

Illustration by scharlay winstenna

Our heart a honeycomb:

With time,
I believe,
With time,
I think,
My heart is the comb,
A comb of honey,
That never resists the sweet,
The sweet that millions,
Millions of bees come to make,
It takes them long,

With time,
The bees never stay,
They take,
Why do they take away?
The sweet,
They run away,
The comb left stranded,
Like empty,
And tasteless rooms,
Rooms for new to come and do the same.

-schone bethal

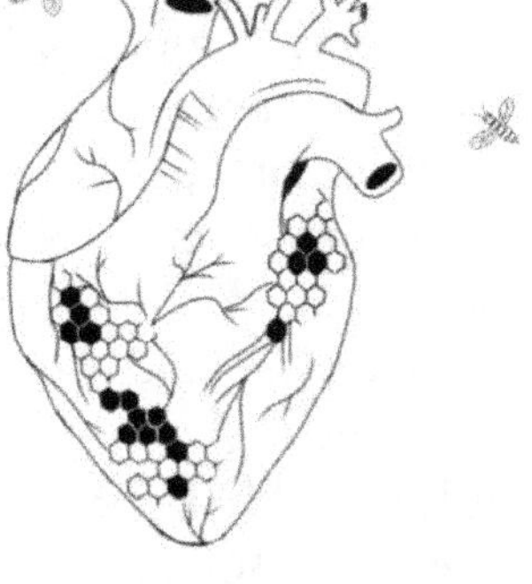

Illustration by scharlay winstenna

Moth and fire:

It's so vague,
I want to sit in the dark,
But towards,
Where I can see the light and flames,
Trace in my fingers,
But I do not want to move close,

It gets vaguer,

Guess I have no wings,
I can move,
Still I'm afraid,
I loved the light,
That makes me frail,
It's so vague.

-desires

-schone bethal

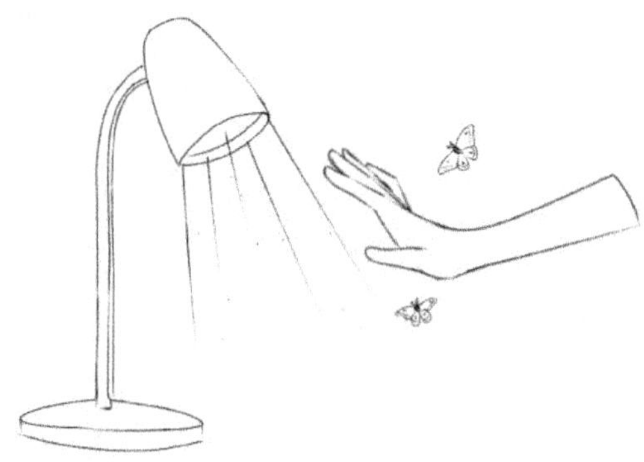

Illustration by scharlay winstenna

Overthinking we pretend:

These sad and dead skulls,
We pretend to wear and hurl,
These masks riot,
Puts the inner skulls on fire,
The actions went over in dire,
The dead comes to pretend burned,
If these bones turning into coal,
Were once sad,
Or dead of our lovers.

- schone bethal

Illustration by scharlay winstenna

Dear deliriousness:

I started to hear footsteps,
Even when no one meant to come,
Does that make me delusional?
Or perceptible enough to expect and run,
I heard voices,
Even when,
No one called me.
Doesn't that makes me delirious,
Because I thought my brain was numb.

-schone bethal

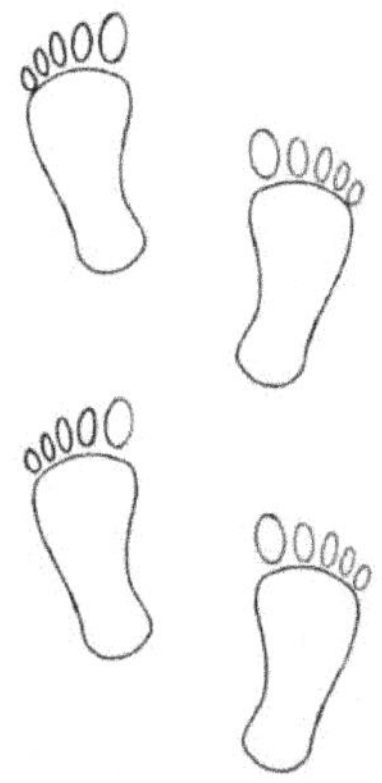

Illustration by scharlay winstenna

Story of magic and tragic:

 I'm the fallen wizard,
 Who failed,
To protect the sanctum,
That is now fallen,

My wand, Lost the light,
That was stolen,

I'm the broken writer,
Who failed ,
To protect the lost,
Who are now fallen ,

My pen,
Lost the enlighten,
That was stolen.

-our halted inner light

- schone bethal

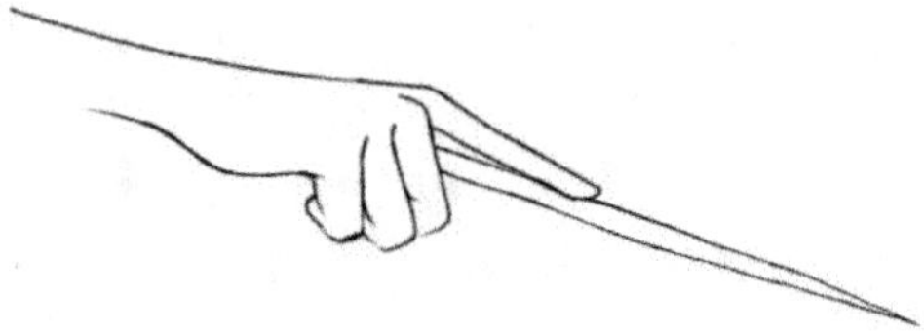

Illustration by scharlay winstenna

Pages of the past:

I am envious,
Of these pages,
Of the books,
They were used,
To went emotions once,
Now that I see and feel,
They dried,
The blurred ink was adored with love,

I aspire to be treated,
Yet my love was turned,
My emotions were locked,
Beneath the visible scars,
That were, once violently inked,
Under the blurred skin,
Cursed to forever reside,
They dried and withered in time,
But scared away their lovers.

-schone bethal

Illustration by scharlay winstenna

Karma said:

Karma said,
It'll be the same tarnished reputation,
Served in the same bowl,
Of the same mold we shaped,
Obliviously imbued within us,
Scratch us to let spill our blood,
When it's the same time,
The same way,
That we decided to shape,
The killing reality for those,
Whom we stabbed,
Spilled their blood,
And those who trusted us,
Blinded eyes and were ready,
To cave for us.

Schone Bethal

Illustration by scharlay winstenna

Rain and tears:

The rain whirled in jealousy,
Striking my existence,
Envious of the amount of tears,
That I shed and drop,
On the thirsty land,
The clouds seem anxious,
Shadowing grey my existence,
Blocking light to enter on my hay,
Envious of how my pounding heart,
Sounded and bled,
The surface beneath me,
Rejoiced and said it was impressed,
But by the uncertain rain,
The dire land cried it was not blessed.

-schone bethal

Illustration by scharlay winstenna

How do we camouflage:

We are the same,
These gravitating places are not,
Lurking and Pacing,
Articulate like a ghost,
Ramifications of our different,
A hundred and Million faces,
Compounding the sky,
Marking the end of the day,
And the halting the land,
Patronizing out different voices,
Becoming swiftly familiar,
Than any other existing face,
How attractive is our magnetic field,
Its consequences brewing,
Making us sinners,
But always moving to find a belief.

-schone bethal

Dear inhumane and stained:

These people pretending,
To possess a divine soul,
Free of sin or a stain,
But shaming the ones,
That might be more pure,
In soul and deeds,
That they don't showcase,

These people inhumane,
They make their soul filthy,
By imposing the stains,
That wouldn't affect anyone,
But their own existence,
That they think is filled,
With grace that only marks their face.

-schone bethal

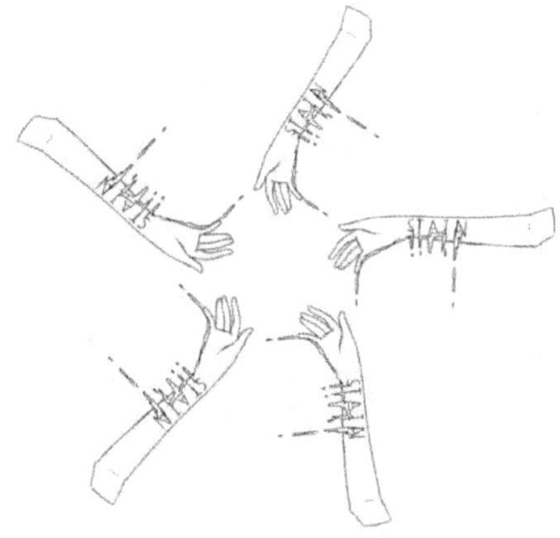

Illustration by scharlay winstenna

Dodging my voice:

I was loud,
When they said,
They couldn't hear me,

They didn't listened,
While I was screaming,
I could hear them turning around on me.

-schone bethal

Illustration by scharlay winstenna

We are greater:

Oh Mighty sky,
When will you fall?
And blend with the land,

To finally,
Let this fallen flesh of yours,
To dwell and stand,

And never fear,
That there's something left,
To, befall and land.

- schone bethal

Illustration by scharlay winstenna

We are special:

Why do you think?
Shooting stars,
Appeared to you?
You wait under the black,
Laying,
To wish,
To discover you
Because,
When you're one of them,
You're not the only one,
Yearning to discover them,
They also seek you,
They wait above the black,
Floating and scrounging,
For you.

- schone bethal

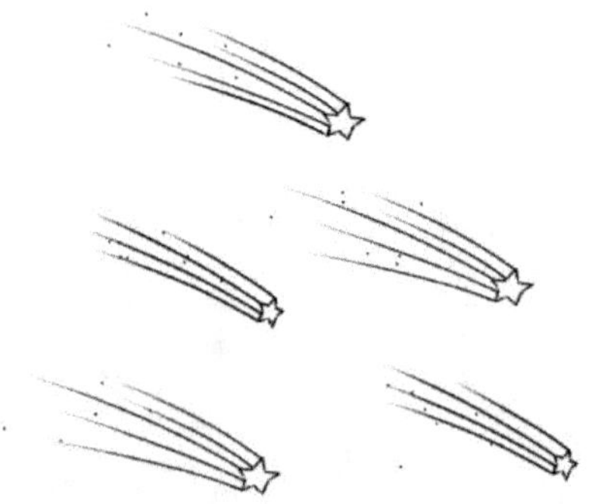

Illustration by scharlay winstenna

Epitome of resilience:

Its okay if no one likes you,
And if there's only you,
Who thrives you,
It's okay if you drifted apart,
And if you outgrew,
To found you,
It's okay if no one believes you,
And if you're confuse,
No one sits beside you,
It's okay if you did something,
And you didn't move on,
But I wish a change to imbue you,
It's okay if you endured,
And never healed,
But consistently try to survive you.

-schone bethal

Illustration by scharlay winstenna

Tempting illusions but no rainbow:

I don't need any rain now, any more,
Wipes away my love for days of light,
So more,

I don't need any new friends, any more,
Lessen my love for real ones by my side,
So more.

- schone bethal

Dear strength:

I may pretend,
To be strongest,
I may pretend to be a haven,
Yet deep down,
I conceal my delicacy,
Under the ocean of tears,
And on corals I depend,
I want to descend,
Into a heaven,
I don't want to depend,
On These moons and stars,
That Seem and shine,
To be fed up of me.

-schone bethal

Illustration by scharlay winstenna

I wandered but I swayed:

I am isolated,
But I find ways,
To wander,
And infiltrate in the raving dark,
Racing to expand,
It also expands like the universe,
But with no shine or any stars to chase,
But invisible fire and terrors,
Burning and haunting my feet and place.

-schone bethal

Illustration by scharlay winstenna

They said my ways depart:

I am blamed,
To be an infernal,
I stood against,
To be on my own way,
I still have the courage,
To rule a kingdom,
I am inborn,
To have the same soul,
I am still by blood a celestial.

-schone bethal

Illustration by scharlay winstenna

I'll still breathe:

Bury me in the ocean,
So that my flesh,
Lives underneath to see,
Through the moving blur,
Dead but to heal,
By the lifeless sun Ray's,
That wouldn't penetrate,
Under the land,
That doesn't moves but stays,
I'll see the sky fall,
One day.

- schone bethal

Illustration by scharlay winstenna

Life ever after:

All the hoax tears,
Those were shed,
Over my dead soil,
Where I'll stay,

They mended all the bones,
And the shattered soul,
That broke,
While I was still awake,

The wet soil from these tears,
Is growing thorns,
That do not hurt me now,
Because I have become stale.

- schone bethal

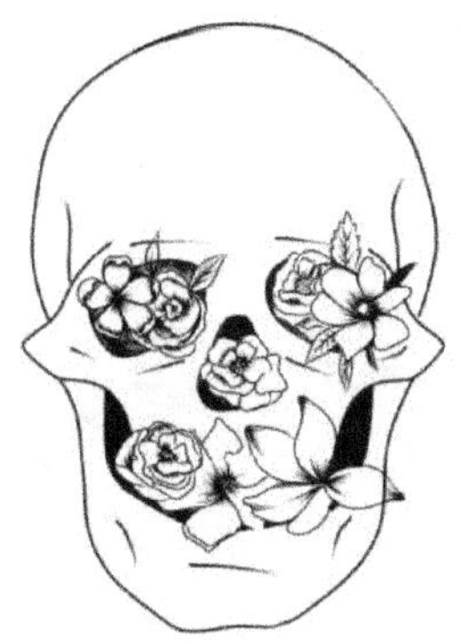

Illustration by scharlay winstenna

Dear death:

I really thought,
Thought that death hurts,
More than life did,
But it did not,
Yes, it doesn't hurts,
It's still all the same,
The thorns grow,
The creeps come,
The land burns my born to coal,
The difference is,
The truth is,
I do not feel that now,
Yes it doesn't hurts,
The life was also killing me,
It doesn't matters above or below now.

-schone bethal

Illustration by scharlay winstenna

Towards home:

Distant was the peace,
Far was every melody,
That had the power to rejoice everything,
Falling and crumbling in chaos within me,

Ran far, far where it was green,
Silent and where I could scream,
Away from the noise of these streets,
Of sins and rushing my howling beats,

The land welcomed me,
Purified and opened every gate,
Hidden like heaven existed there for me,
Horns and lies of hell silenced in a fleet,

In the right home it felt,
With a collusion of my empty soul,
And the nature that was ready to fill me,
With patience that this world couldn't be,

The golden hour seemed different,
Created the beams of true light,
That everyone is blinded to not see,
And the appealing rhythm, no one has ever felt.

-schone bethal.

Illustration by scharlay winstenna

THIRTEENTH HOUR

TIMELESS FLIGHTS OF SOUL BEYOND THE SECRET SKIES OF LOVE

FALSE GOD: LOVE

By all appearances, we all know where this complicated notion of lost being delineated, is leading us to. Well, it can never be the last thing but it is supposedly one of the things on the rim where being lost in, is just inexorable and relatively unforeseeable for the soul. Yes, we are entirely deviating towards a phase where we are lost while seeking LOVE and affection unaware of its repercussions and what it might cost us. Where we inaugurate ourselves to worship LOVE and get lost in the brewing sentiments, and start believing that it is everything eternal and beyond. But I emphasize LOVE as false God with no reality. We cannot debunk the fact that LOVE nurtures and makes us cognize those beautiful sentiments that are never felt anywhere before. Consequently, we can also neither defy the fact that those pretentious and beautiful clouds of feelings seem to dissipate eventually and that is where exactly we realize we are lost in the search for love that is also itself illusionary, which has no base to protect us when we fall. We craved for it and we relentlessly embark on a solemn mission to still crave it even when it left us weak and delicate enough to break. The worst part of loving someone and then expecting that in return is the epitome of being lost while finding the lost. Yes, we cannot rescue ourselves when bogus and hoax hopes attract us and the pulls that only deem to throw us into the black holes that wipe us out entirely. From where there is no way to return but to be lost forever.

Again as reiterated before, fake affections and attractive pulls shouldn't have to be entitled as the scape goats but our stubborn hearts that still wanted to move towards them and leaves to fly without the soul that always have the power to imbues us with patience, techniques of survival, helps us learn to fly the right way, give us new pair of wings, settles, seeds itself, waters itself and thrives infinitely.

Innocent flights:

This doomed heart,
Dreams of flying,
And to be above the haze,
Without the immortal wings,
Of the utmost promising soul
Even though in every flight,
It faces crash,
Overloaded with passengers,
Without the help,
Of the winds of soul,
It risks, being in that phase.

- schone bethal

Illustration by scharlay winstenna

Without spacesuit towards your stars:

Leaving to find you,
Listened to the heart that rules,
Packed the brain to be numb,
Was leaving my soul behind,
Stranded alone for you,
In the midst of that journey,
I suffocated and realized,
That you never alarmed me about a downfall,
While crossing and enduring,
The limits for you, Just to retrieve you,
I was lost,
I con my soul,
Cut my real wings,
And buried my protection,
Just for you.

-schone bethal

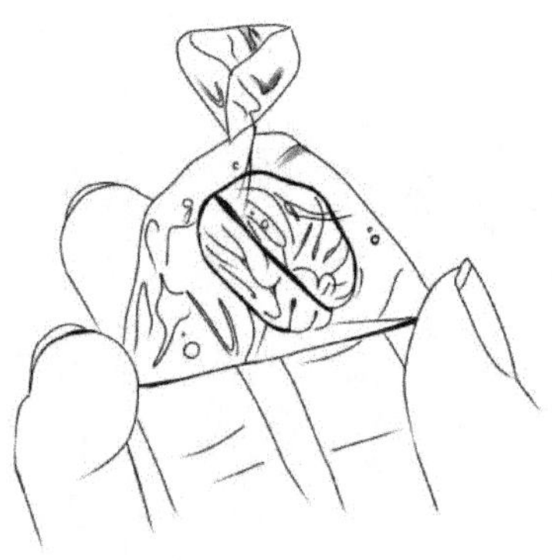

Illustration by scharlay winstenna

Healing from a thousand miles:

The infinite universe, Preserved In your form,
I reckoned from far away,
Lying beneath your skin,
Not everyone can see,
And prey,

I'm ready to blend my spirit,
I'm like a planet,
Let me revolve around yours,
Because Where I dwell is not less than a Hell,
It sores,

You have the stars, Fulgent than mine,
Your touch can heal,
My gloomy heart,
From a thousand miles,
In just a feel.

- schone bethal

Illustration by scharlay winstenna

Beautiful vows:

And, we dreamt in the daylight,
To muse together with stars,
And dance until moon became closer,
In the dead of the night,
It never came to fruition,
By any chance,
Because we ended up being lost,
Fell again,
In each other's sight.

- schone bethal

Illustration by scharlay winstenna

A half written story:

The revived soul,
Of my clipped wings,
Still constant and imprisoned,
But wills to flee,
Towards your Eden,
It still sends the invincible winds,
Arousing every warrior,
To combat with,
To prevail,
And unlock my wings,
In despair and exile,
Make me free,
To fulfill the destiny,
That you wished,
In the garden of eve,
But told me to wait,
To not break out and heal.

-schone bethal

Illustration by scharlay winstenna

Stuck with you:

Rather to be lost,
In our harsh past,
I'd like to be stuck,
In the present,
With your delicate palms.

Rather to unlock,
The obscure future,
I'd like to be stuck,
In the timeless moments,
With your delicate soul.

-schone bethal

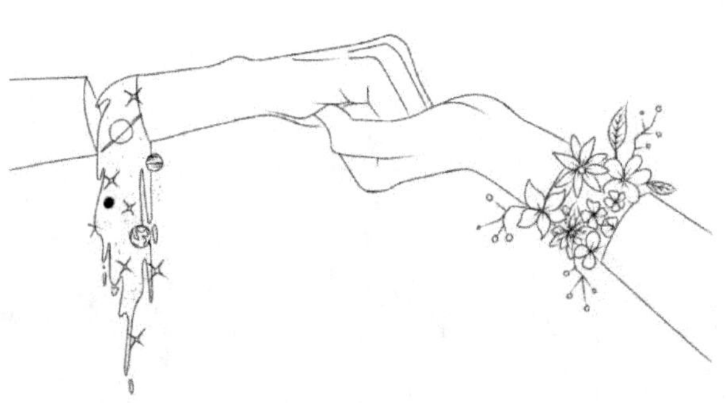

Illustration by scharlay winstenna

Journey of our faulted stars:

Can I believe?
That you are,
The shooting star,

Because I am being nurtured,
In the dark,
To live a thousand lives,

By the moonlight,
From across so far,

Can I believe?
You conjure,
The moonbow above me,

Because I'm being lured,
To embrace,
Your ever shade of dark,

To escape on it with you,
To run so far.

- schone bethal

Love for poison:

You've been thriving on my heart,
Like a garden of daisies,
Often poised ivies now,

My tears,
Those have stopped,
To shed outside now,

Are constantly raining,
Inside me,
Giving your poisoned garden a bliss now,

To tear me,
Apart one day,
Why do I hesitate to stop you now?

- schone bethal

Illustration by scharlay winstenna

Two hearts igniting the same rhythm:

You fly, and soar,
In the songs,
Of love,
Chirping with the bracing wind,
I dive deep,
And swim in the songs,
Of love,
Harmonizing with hidden corals.

- schone bethal

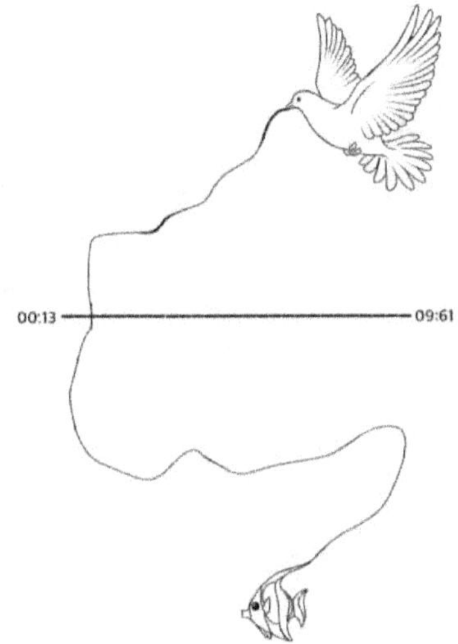

Illustration by scharlay winstenna

Wishes upon stars:

An empty bulb,
And a full moon,

An empty mind,
And a heart,

Full of you,

Gloomy world, desolated,
The blurred gleams, not enough,

Moon and my heart, colliding,
To beam my naive stars,

Wishing for you.

- schone bethal

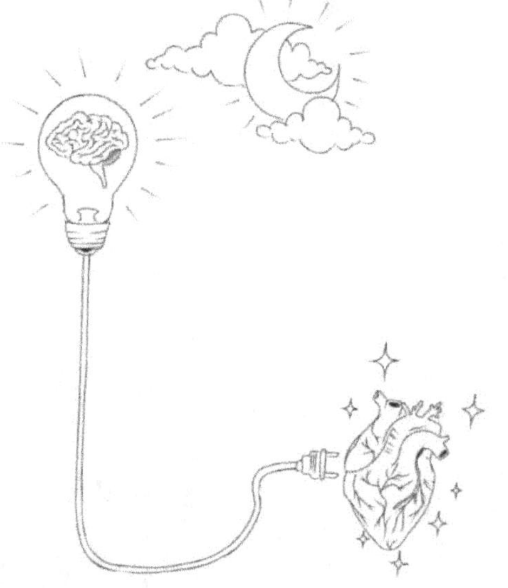

Illustration by scharlay winstenna

Immature love:

We are songs,
To each other,

Beautiful,
Filled with colors,

Matching beats,
Burning lovers,

Destined to end,
Failed to impress forever,

Time is paused,
Because, we were recording covers.

- schone bethal

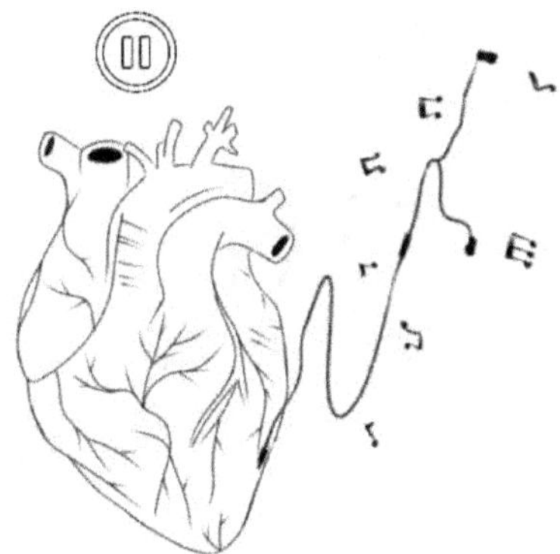

Illustration by scharlay winstenna

Dreadful dreams of tears part 1:

I've been sailing,
This creaky boat, forever,
Over your kingdom,
Of dreadful,
And deep waters,

I'm certain,
If I drown,
I won't be recovered,
I'm still thriving,
On uncertain hopes,
To reach the shores,

And rejoice,
That I survived,
A ship wreck,
That cursed,
The oceans of my heart forever.

- schone bethal

Illustration by scharlay winstenna

Dreadful dreams of tears part 2:

I have returned,
Back,
In a dream this time,
But Breath I lack,
But why,
Why is it crystal,
And glitter around me,
Your kingdoms that was haunting me,
Is finally pure now that I see,
Is it really a dream I see,
I'm drowning,
I reckoned,
I don't have the creaky boat,
I was sailing all along in grief,
But I see you clear,
Reaching me,
Your divine spirit ready to rescue me,
But you're screaming,
To wake me,
Into the subtle reality,
Where you didn't save me.

- schone bethal

Illustration by scharlay winstenna

Ungrateful and cruel:

Am I that favorite chapter?
Of the darkest book,
You read to complain every night,

The one you said,
That protects you,
From falling into the sleep that frights,

The one you said,
That would bring dark terrors,
To life,

You're just ungrateful,
I have been this long,
By your side,

My pages, Had a title,
But you still name it 'cruel'

- schone bethal

Illustration by scharlay winstenna

Dark rituals of love:

Will you perform?
A dark ritual,
Tonight in the twilight,
I sacrifice myself,
Under the hare moon,
And you revive me,
With the blood,
Dripping from your soul,
Crippling and absorbing,
Travelling Down,
Into the land filled with holes,
Void with Emptiness,
Rewriting the buried past,
Written for us to separate,
But unlike our hearts,
Where we grow now,
Like where we were born,
Always to fall, but stay.

-schone bethal

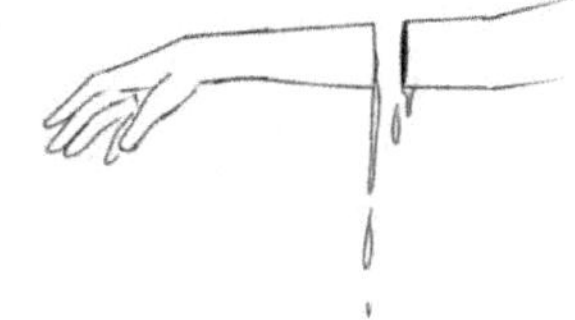

Illustration by scharlay winstenna

Burying flashbacks:

I would save our memories,
In Polaroid,
Than on screen,
I don't want to delete,

I would want to burn them,
Feel the flames on my skin,
When you disappear,
While I scream,

I'd feel like I've been told,
Burning in hell,
Paying for someone's else's sin,
Wrenching in memories.

-assassination of memories

- schone bethal

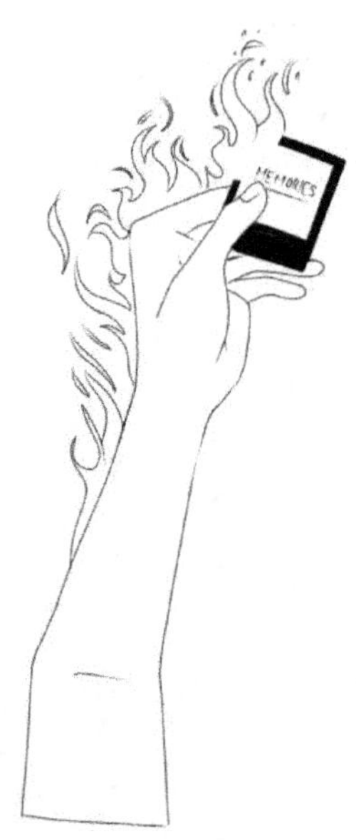

Illustration by scharlay winstenna

Your raving revelations:

I have become prone,
To slip every time,
From these frozen scars,
Grooved on my skin,
You thought you blessed,
To make me cold and shone,
But you cursed me to break,
I flipped every time when I lurked.

- schone bethal

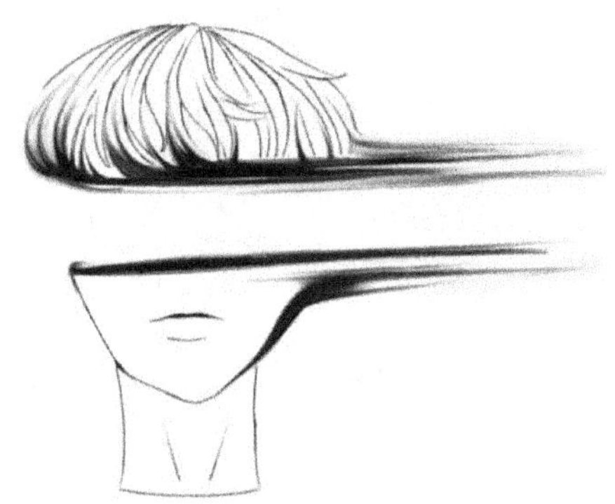

Illustration by scharlay winstenna

Promises of the nature:

We were so miry,
But,
Not even a flow of wind,
Even a flinch,
Won't compromise,

To let us be one,

I'm conflicted by the examples,
This universe promises,
When the different clouds forged together,
To be one,
Rejuvenate the wonders of thunderstorms,

Together as one,

Their rain drops, amalgamating,
Into an ocean,

It's always one.

- schone bethal

Illustration by scharlay winstenna

A tale of two rivers:

The two different rivers,
Of our bridled emotions,
Halted to flow between us,
They were already ceasing,
They were running so slow,
I surmised now,
There were just dreams reflecting,
Only pain could've helped,
To make it strong and fast so more,
By shedding the tears of pain,
From both the sides of the distance,
Of the true emotions,
That could create a bridge so pure,
But not alone this time can do assure,
Yet the two rivers might connect us,
But the chances of mixing,
Never been as deep,
As our rivers though.

-schone bethal

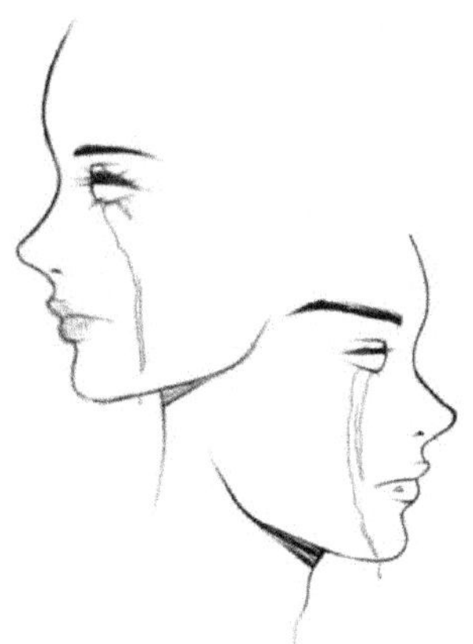

Illustration by scharlay winstenna

Ungrateful love:

Cried a river,
Been hanging upside down,
Just For you,
But you still had the nerve,
To utter and complain,
That you died with thirst,
Being delusive but wanting,
A castle made in the air,
Complaining and wanting help,
No way to swim down to the cores,
That my river doesn't flow right,
You thought so much,
But you felt so little,
Faking it till it made you contenrt,
Been your ride to the planes of the grass,
Took you to the fields of Wheat,
Travelled for you,
But you still died with thirst,
For not the water this time,
You craved the winds,
No way to fly above,
You cried,
That those fields don't flow,
You thought so much,
But you felt so little.

-schone bethal

Illustration by scharlay winstenna

Persuasive spells:

I stayed up,
Talking to the moon,
You were the dream,
Ceasing to bloom,
You persuaded me to think,
You were the source,
Of my every gloom,
This truth was,
Meant to never groom,
Scared about my affinity for you,
When the light,
Yet not just the dark of you,
Nurturing my empty soul,
That was always you.

-

Illustration by scharlay winstenna

Traitor reflectors:

We write on the mirrors,
Filling it to vent suffering of the inner,
Smudging our true sides and shimmer,
These mirrors pledged,
To show me the real glitter,
Instead it blurred my vision and other purposes,
Arousing love for fake beauty and glimmer,
I think these mirrors are the real killers.

-schone bethal

Illustration by scharlay winstenna

Stole my heart but left your mark:

I was riding,
But I never went far,
You were flying,
But you left across the stars,

I was searching,
Your dependent soul,
You left for me,
To remove its scars,

What do I do,
With these two souls,
Both lurking in fear,
Because you had the two hearts,

One mine,
And other is yours,
Amalgamated into strongest wings,
That took you afar,

I saw the window obscuring my rendezvous,
With droplets that were supposed to be shed,
From my heavy heart, yet they fall inside,
Weighing my heart to call me back from afar.

-schone bethal

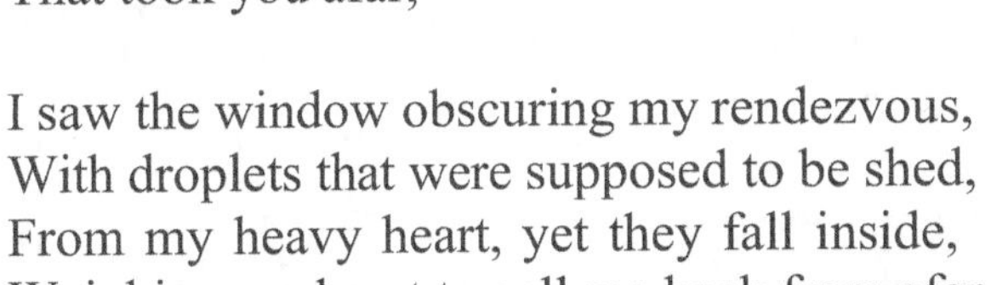

Illustration by scharlay winstenna

Your world:

I'm dubious if I exist,
In this stellar world of yours,
There are many ivories and sparkles,
I can vividly see,
No wonder If they exist,
to Cherish you Devine morality,
Visible clouds as if scars,
Vibrant but vexed auroras,
Darker the waters appear,
Breeze is spellbinding yet dry,
I heard,
Sublime the foundation is,
I want to venture the skydive,
To heal the scars in disguise of clouds,
I wish to transform the oceans,
That will stay everlasting,
I'd like to be invisible,
If you seem to shrug me,
But set me apart,
I'll be the same, I'll be me,
I'm better than the enormous,
Fires of your sun,
I'll better than the withered winds,
That shivers your skies,

At last, I'll make you happier, When I rain.

- schone bethal

Illustration by scharlay winstenna

Your world part 2:

In the midst of wilderness,
I found an oasis,
An oasis of love,
That fills my cup,
Lilac skies above the dessert,
Fleeting bliss,
Enchanting enough,
Your world held an Incandescent love,
Would I ever be enough?
Floating the waves are,
In your ocean heart,
With wrecks of love,
That yearns to last,
Oblivious of all sorrows,
Those lie beneath,
Deep beneath an ocean off eternity,
All other worlds do not collide, Like you and me,
Your gravity pulls me deep,
Reviving the flames that once burned me,
All my remains drifted off,
To the place,
Where endearment revolves,
Now my mind slips its way across,
The thoughts,
And the heart ignite a vulnerable spot,
And I know your world,
Will be better than the winds,

At last, more happier, When you rain.

- misha ilyas

Illustration by scharlay winstenna

You were lying:

Your heart Complained,
To study the scars,
Grooved on my deserted skin,
When you read my empty mind,
The nightmares you said it showed you,
You were just lying,
That your heart was blind,
Because you never learned how to read,
You were just lying,
My brain was empty and revived this time,
The brails in form of scars,
Were shinning and starred in a while,
You said were cursed,
While touching mine,
You were astonished to see my bright,
Or your eyes got jealous and blind.

-schone bethal

Two different worlds:

Your moon bled,
Where my earth cried,

Your stars shine,
Where my darkness rise,

Your way appears,
Where my road only longs to thrive,

You're part of the same universe,
Where my existence silently survives.

- schone bethal

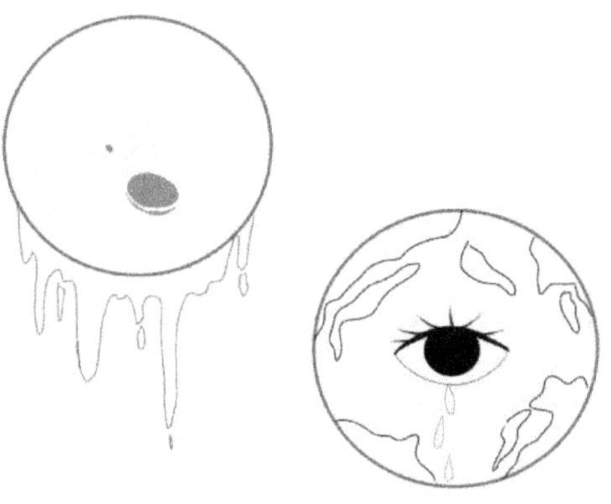

Illustration by scharlay winstenna

Illustration of your past and my present:

I made a new art,
Art free of your reality and cruelty,

I hid cruelty,
Cruelty just to free myself and you,

The past, I mean here,
Is the cruelty, the present is the art,

I accepted it,
Draw and be in present, with a new you.

I adore it,
I see it burning from afar.

-schone bethal

Freezing and melting:

I try to fly above for you,
It blinds and melts my sights,

i keep touching cold darkness beneath me ,
That freezes my light,

-schone bethal

Appreciation:

I appreciated the art,
And the symphonies of your melodies,
Because it appealed you,

You judged mine,
Judged mine without cognizing,
My taste was only you,

Your existence,
Your existence was harmonizing to me,
You were the art to me,

It was my fault,
My choice made me see,
Were you appealing like an illusion to me.

-schone bethal

Illustration by scharlay winstenna

Fake promises:

Your promises sparkle,
But they are empty,
They sound like apologies,
Like the fire of my soul,
But your promises shun me,
Stranded in your cold ,
Unlike my burning but honest soul,
You promise to die for me,
But do you promise to live for me?

-Schone bethal

Illustration by scharlay winstenna

Goodbyes:

The broken clouds,
So sublime,
At the dusk they shine!
They outburst with the last shine of day,
Will they move on and bring the night?
At the dusk they shine!
On the Sun's good bye,

The broken heart,
So terrifying,
At the dolour it cries!
It outbursts with the distress,
Coming for it to check if it's dead or alive?
At the dolour, it cries!
On the lover's good bye.

- schone bethal

Illustration by scharlay winstenna

Shrugged in the twilight:

It kept me awake,
The fear of your face,

The night was tricked,
It triggered us to break,

While you were conjuring thoughts,
Pondering about a beguiling fate,

Star gazing the starless sky,
Till late,

I'm your 6 am alarm,
You thwacked me to make my sleep elate,

And defied me,
Who cared about you and didn't irate.

-you're my midnight sun

- schone bethal

Sheer reality:

May be you loved writing,
Stories of our thriller fiction,
In which you deemed to kill me,
As a character that was purely main,
But to you was a piece of plot twist,
Used but was called boring and frail,
My fate ignored by your dear readers,
They might not reckon,
That it was assassinated decisively,
Written to just get erased,
Reciprocated with many mistakes,
But was able to conjured more stories,
With which you succumbed to take stakes.

-our folklore

-schone bethal

Love as a self taught language:

May be Love is a language,
A language having beautiful semblance,
Just like a mother language,
Self taught and natural,
From within and through the rinse,
Of bond strengthening by a contact,
With people of different hearts,
And exhilaratingly factious voices,
Getting familiar through bits and pieces,
Accumulating to live and keep seeking,
That's how we spoke to keep living,
That's how we love to keep breathing.

-natural

-schone bethal

Illustration by scharlay winstenna

Expectations charged with crimes of gluttony:

In the midst,
Of my various hollowed expectations,
Mentioning it one by one with celerity,
The list was long,
I got my desirous tongue thirsted,
It got bit excruciatingly between the teeth,
That I wished to laugh out loud,
At the same things you did,
The sharp pain killed,
My sheer sobriety,
That has always been called,
My blunt gluttony.

- schone bethal

Illustration by scharlay winstenna

Defied forever:

The sunshine,
Reflecting through the mirror,
Making your Ray's,
More powerful,
To burn me forever,

Like love,
You craved from others,
With dark power,
That slaughtered,
Your true lovers.

- schone bethal

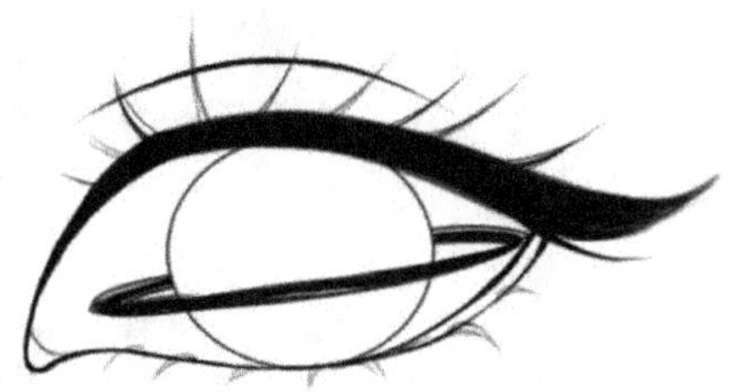

Illustration by scharlay winstenna

Your illicit dreams:

Your frowned eyebrows,
Your voided eyes,
Showed the Terror,
That you concealed,
That you sewed,
Behind your lips,
That once wore red shades,
And burning fire,
Those were always still,
The world warned you,
To not go down that road,
 But you fought to rule,
Yet you were caught too soon.

-schone bethal

Illustration by scharlay winstenna

Sewing time in the wells of dime:

I'd rather turn the clock backwards,
Instead of a wishing to go forward,
But I'd trade my soul, With your wish,
Of turning backwards, You were ready before,
To not wait for my hand,
And you know how my soul,
Will linger and slow, It would disintegrate,
My new timeless soul mirroring into the well,
Of gleaming water shining alone,
We came ok aboard,
Where souls flows but not the time,
That is always lost,
Echoes souls instead of voices,
Faulted with greed and thunderstorms,
Showed my foreseen heart first,
As empty and with holes,
Its water turned black and stroke,
Because of the soul echoing down,
Foretold a secret,
That it never existed in the unseen past,
Only Pain It showed,
I see you your soul grew even In the backwards,
Rather than shrinking,
I realize it will always be you,
Who flew with the freedom tunes?
Where I'll be endeavoring to change the future now,
Trying to change the ending,
Hoping it wouldn't be cruel,
But my Peter losing your Wendy,
Would be the smoothest loose.

-schone bethal

Illustration by scharlay winstenna

-EPILOGUE-

"The ones that are lost and go beyond time

will always find themselves."

-schone bethal